DOWN IN THE BUNKER

A JOURNEY OF FAITH, FEAR, AND FINDING HOPE

BY:

LOVESUN PARENT

Dedication

To those with a servant's heart—
who choose compassion over comfort,
who see the unseen,
who hear the cries of the forgotten,
who walk alongside the weary,
and who labor in love for the least of these.
May your faith remain steadfast,
your light never dim,
and your calling be met with grace.
This book is for you—
the ones who serve not for recognition,
but for the glory of God's kingdom.

ACKNOWLEDGMENT

With a heart full of gratitude, I extend my deepest thanks to my family—my foundation, my strength, and my constant source of love.

To my beloved husband and life partner, your support, love, and belief in me have carried me through every chapter of this journey. To our beautiful children, who bring light and purpose to my days, you are my greatest blessings.

To my incredible parents, thank you for instilling in me the values of faith, resilience, and service. To my siblings, who have stood by my side through every season, your love and encouragement mean more than words can express.

To my dear friends—your prayers, encouragement, and belief in me have been a source of strength. Thank you for always reminding me of my purpose.

And to my Mount Olive Baptist Church family, thank you for seeing in me what God has placed within. Your guidance and encouragement have helped me embrace my spiritual gifts and walk boldly in my calling.

I am grateful beyond measure to each of you. This book is as much yours as it is mine.

CONTENTS

INTRODUCTION

The Day Everything Changed

Some moments split life into a before and after.

One night in Kabul, the Taliban struck. Explosions shattered the silence, gunfire ripped through the air, and the ground trembled beneath me. In an instant, what had always been a distant threat became terrifyingly real.

I didn't know if I would make it out alive.

Fear clawed at my throat, but in those terrifying hours, I discovered something I never expected—when everything else crumbles, faith is the only thing that holds.

This book isn't just about surviving a terrorist attack—it's about holding onto faith when life unravels. It's about living fully, even when fear tries to take everything. If you've ever searched for peace in the midst of chaos, this book is for you.

My story is an invitation to step deeper into faith, trust, and a life anchored in something unshakable.

When you're down in the bunker, you discover what truly holds you up.

A Night of Terror

The night felt ordinary—until it wasn't.

I was on the treadmill, my feet pounding against the belt, sweat pooling at my lower back. My body ached, but I pushed through. That was my nature—always pushing, always enduring. But then, through the hum of the machine, I heard it. A whisper stirred in my spirit, quiet but undeniable:

"Baby girl, it's too late to be here."

I slowed down, my natural stubbornness ready to argue back, but something inside me stopped. I couldn't explain it, but I listened. I stepped off the treadmill, grabbed my towel, and walked out of the gym into the cool, quiet night.

My office was just across the way—cold, empty, and scattered with boxes from our closeout. I flipped on the light and sat down, catching my breath. My heart was still racing from the workout, but there was something else too. A heaviness. A feeling I couldn't shake.

I called home. I needed to hear my babies' voices, their laughter, their life. But as we talked, a chill crept over me, the kind that makes the hairs on your arms stand tall. It was as if someone was watching me. Then the voice came again, gentle but insistent:

"Baby girl, it's too late to be here."

This time, I didn't hesitate. I said my goodbyes, turned off the lights, and walked out, my pace quickening with an urgency I couldn't explain. As I passed the gym, I took the long way back to my residence, veering away from the restaurant and garden. Normally, I would've stopped, maybe chatted with a colleague or waved at familiar faces. But not tonight. Tonight, the voice guided me forward.

The five-minute walk felt longer than usual. My feet moved, but my mind raced. Something was off.

When I reached my studio apartment, I exhaled, letting my body finally relax. I scrolled through my phone absentmindedly as I stripped off my clothes. I turned on the shower, letting the water warm up, my mind drifting. Just as I was about to step in—

Boom.

A sound so powerful it felt like the world had cracked open.

The lights went out. The air itself seemed to shatter. I stood there, frozen, my breath caught somewhere between my ribs. The silence that followed wasn't real silence—it was the kind that rings in your ears, the kind that holds a question you don't want answered.

Then, the night erupted.

Gunfire. A relentless, deafening storm of rounds slicing through the darkness. I dropped to the floor, pressing my body against the cold ground, my heart hammering against my ribs.

This wasn't just an explosion. This was an attack.

And I was in the middle of it.

The Chaos, Fear, and Uncertainty of Survival

I mustered the courage to open my door. My hands trembled as I reached for the handle, my breath shallow, my heart pounding against my ribs.

Standing in the dimly lit hallway was my chief of security—a tall, broad-shouldered former British soldier, the man responsible for keeping our USAID project safe from the Taliban. He was usually a calm, unshaken presence, but even in the darkness, I could see the tension in his face.

In a voice barely above a whisper, I uttered, *"Are we under attack?"* as if I needed someone to confirm that this wasn't just a nightmare.

He didn't hesitate. *"Run. Now."*

His words snapped something inside me into action. Like we had rehearsed in our security drills, I turned and ran. The gunfire outside grew louder, closer. My bare feet pounded against the cold concrete as I sprinted past the four other units, while gripping onto my sneakers and grab bag. Each step felt heavier than the last. I didn't dare look back.

For those who have never seen a bunker, imagine a small, suffocating concrete structure with two rows of benches, built to fit no more than twelve people. It was designed to protect us from bombs and gunfire, but at that moment, it felt more like a tomb. At just over 5 feet, I had to hunch and crawl my way in. There was no room to stand, no space to move.

We crammed inside, our bodies pressed together, knees knocking against each other in the darkness. The air was thick with fear. The sound of my own ragged breathing mixed with the chaos outside—gunfire tearing through the night, explosions rumbling in the distance.

I was naked under the bathrobe I had barely managed to grab. My body shook violently, uncontrollably, from more than just the cold. Terror gripped me from the inside out.

I sat there, trembling, tears blurring my vision, my breath coming in short, panicked gasps. I wasn't ready. I wasn't ready to die.

My thoughts raced to my children—their faces, their laughter, their futures without me. My heart ached for my mother. I could see her pain, the weight of my absence crushing her. The thought of her receiving the news—of the phone call that would change everything—made the fear unbearable.

I wept silently, then loudly as my body shook with the weight of it all.

This was it. This was how my story would end.

Faith as an Anchor in the Storm

In that bunker, as the hours crawled toward daylight and the battle raged on outside, something unexpected happened—peace showed its head, as gentle as a dove.

It didn't flood in all at once. It came in waves—between whispered prayers, in the quiet surrender of my soul to something greater than my fear. My body still trembled, my heart still pounded, but deep within, a stillness began to settle. My prayers weren't frantic pleas for survival; they became prayers of remembrance.

I thought of all the times God had carried me.

I had spent my life praying over my work, asking God to use me to serve the least of these. I could have chosen a different path, but my faith had led me here—to the margins, to the forgotten, to the places where justice and mercy were needed most. And even now, in the middle of chaos, I knew my work wasn't finished.

Looking back, I can see how the bunker became more than just a shelter. It became a reflection of the stories I had read in scripture—stories of faith tested by fire, of trust forged in trial.

Like Daniel in the lion's den (*Daniel 6:16-23*), I was surrounded by danger beyond my control, waiting to see if I would make it out alive. The walls of that concrete space might not have held roaring beasts, but death loomed just as near. And like Daniel, I waited in the darkness, unsure of my fate but trusting in the One who held it.

Like Shadrach, Meshach, and Abednego in the fiery furnace (*Daniel 3:16-27*), I was engulfed by a different kind of fire—a world ablaze with violence and destruction. They stood firm, knowing that even if God did not rescue them, He was still sovereign. And I, too, had to find that trust.

And like Jesus in the storm (*Mark 4:35-41*), I was caught in a tempest that threatened to consume me. The disciples panicked as the waves crashed around them, but Jesus slept—calm, unshaken—because He knew the storm had no power over Him. I was anything but calm in that bunker, but I longed for that kind of faith—the faith that trusts even when the waters rage.

The bunker itself became a symbol—a place of trial, of waiting, of surrender.

And yet, God was there.

His promises whispered through my fear, through the pounding of my heart, through the trembling of my hands:

- *When you pass through the waters, I will be with you; and when you pass through the rivers, they will not sweep over you. When you walk through the fire, you will not be burned; the flames will not set you ablaze.* — Isaiah 43:2

- *The Lord is my light and my salvation—whom shall I fear? The Lord is the stronghold of my life—of whom shall I be afraid?* — Psalm 27:1

- *Even though I walk through the darkest valley, I will fear no evil, for You are with me; Your rod and Your staff, they comfort me.* — Psalm 23:4

I inhaled deeply, letting those words root themselves in my spirit.

If this was my time, I was at peace. But if God had more for me to do, then I would walk out of that bunker knowing—without a shadow of a doubt—that I was still here for a reason.

I had prayed for a life of meaning. I had prayed to be used as a vessel for change. And there, in the middle of war, in the darkness of that bunker, I realized—faith was the only thing keeping me upright.

God was with me.

And He had never left.

PART ONE

THE BUNKER
AND THE BATTLE WITHIN

THE PHYSICAL
AND SPIRITUAL BUNKER

Surviving the Immediate Aftermath

The moment they cleared us to leave the bunker, my body refused to move at first. My mind understood that the siege was over, but something deep within me wasn't convinced. I had spent 12 hours in that space—hunched, trembling, praying. My body had absorbed every explosion, every round of gunfire, every whispered plea for survival.

But now, the door opened, and I was expected to step out. I forced myself to stand, my legs unsteady beneath me. As I took my first steps outside, the air felt thick, heavy with the remnants of smoke and death. The stench of burnt flesh clung to everything. The camp, once a place of routine and familiarity, had been transformed into something unrecognizable.

The gym where I had been just hours before—where I had heard that soft whisper telling me to leave—was now nothing more than charred remains. The treadmill I had been running on was melted, warped into something grotesque. The ground was littered with debris, soaked in the destruction left behind.

I tried to look away, but my eyes refused to obey.

This was the moment no one prepares you for—the part of survival that isn't about dodging bullets or finding shelter. It's the moment you realize you have lived while others have not. It's the part where you carry the weight of what your eyes have seen, what your body has endured.

Trauma doesn't leave quietly. It takes root in your body, in your muscles, in the very air you breathe. The body remembers what the mind tries to forget. The tremors in my hands, the sudden shallow breaths, the way my heart pounded at the slightest noise—these were the echoes of that night, the proof that survival comes at a cost.

And yet, stepping out of that bunker meant something.

It reminded me of Noah and the ark, of how he had waited for the waters to recede, sending out a dove to see if the storm had passed (*Genesis 8:8-12*). When the dove finally returned with an olive leaf, it was proof that dry land was near—that the world had not been lost to destruction.

I didn't feel like I had survived the flood—only its wreckage. But stepping out of that bunker was my olive leaf, a sign the storm had passed, even if I didn't feel safe yet.

God had carried me through.

I was changed, but I was still here.

And that had to mean something.

The Power of Faith Under Fire

Faith is easy when life is predictable—when prayers are answered in ways we recognize, when safety is certain, when struggles feel manageable. But faith under fire? That's something different.

That kind of faith is not about rehearsed prayers or Sunday morning devotionals. It is raw, desperate, and tested in ways no one can prepare for. It is the kind of faith that clings to God—not because everything is okay, but because there is nothing else left to hold onto.

When the attack on the compound began, my body reacted before my mind could catch up. The explosion rattled through my bones, the air itself seemed to split apart, and the night was swallowed by the chaos of gunfire and destruction. My first instinct was survival. My second was prayer.

I didn't pray for miracles. I prayed for presence.

I prayed to feel God near, to remember His promises, to quiet the terror rising in my chest. And in that bunker, through the gunfire, through the suffocating fear, I held onto what I knew to be true:

God was with me. Even in this.

Faith under fire is not about having no fear—it's about choosing to believe even when fear is screaming in your ears.

Look at Job—a man who lost everything and still declared, *"Though He slay me, yet will I trust in Him."* (*Job 13:15*). That kind of faith is terrifying because it requires surrender. It acknowledges that God's will is bigger than our understanding.

I think of Paul and Silas in prison, beaten and chained, yet still singing praises (*Acts 16:25-26*). They had no guarantee of deliverance, yet their faith did not waver.

I wasn't singing. I wasn't boldly declaring victory. I was trembling. I was crying. But I was still believing. And sometimes, that is enough.

There's a reason why scripture speaks so often of refining fire—because faith that has not been tested has not been strengthened. The fire strips away illusions, burns off what is weak, and leaves behind only what is real.

That night, I realized faith is not just what we profess in moments of peace—it's what we practice in the trenches.

And faith under fire? It is costly. It requires everything.

But it is also unshakable. Because once you've clung to God in the darkest moment of your life, you will never again doubt that He is there.

Fear, Faith, and the Human Spirit

Wrestling with Mortality and Fear

Fear has a way of settling into the bones after survival. It doesn't disappear when the gunfire stops or when the evacuation orders come. It lingers—tightening in the chest at unexpected moments, whispering doubts in the silence, creeping into spaces where peace used to reside.

I had many sleepless nights after the attack. Even when I was physically safe, my mind was still trapped in that moment. The first night I laid in bed before being evacuated, I expected relief. Instead, the silence was deafening.

Eerie. Overwhelming. Unnatural.

After a night filled with explosions and gunfire, silence became its own kind of terror. The absence of chaos felt wrong, as if something else—something worse—was waiting just beyond the quiet. My body remained on high alert, every sound amplified, every shadow suspect.

And then came the realization of loss.

One of my gym workout partners had been killed in that very same gym. The garden, where I had avoided stopping to chat just hours before the attack, had become a graveyard. Friends had died in the restaurant, their laughter silenced in an instant. The pool table where we had once gathered for lighthearted games was now shattered into pieces, a reflection of everything that had been taken.

Surviving was not just about making it out alive. It was about facing the unbearable weight of knowing that others had not.

That weight was heavier than I could have ever imagined. It pressed on my chest, made my breaths shallow, and wrapped itself around my thoughts like an iron grip. I struggled to grasp the reality that I had lived while others had died, that I had been spared when I easily could have been one of the names whispered in mourning.

This is what survivor's guilt does—it asks unanswerable questions. *Why them and not me? What makes my life worthy of continuation while theirs were cut short?*

But in my wrestling, in my sleepless nights, in my grief, I had to confront a deeper truth—one that faith demands of us: death is not the end.

As a believer, I had always known this. But knowing something in theory and walking through it in reality are two different things. I had stood in church and recited scripture, yet here I was, struggling to reconcile the pain of loss with the promise of eternity.

I found comfort in the words of 1 Thessalonians 4:13-14:

> *"Brothers and sisters, we do not want you to be uninformed about those who sleep in death, so that you do not grieve like the rest of mankind, who have no hope. For we believe that Jesus died and rose again, and so we believe that God will bring with Jesus those who have fallen asleep in him."*

These words didn't erase my pain, but they anchored me. The people I lost were not gone—they had just gone ahead. Their stories didn't end in the fire and destruction of that night. They lived on in eternity, in the presence of the God who wipes away every tear.

The heaviness in my heart remained, but faith gave me a way forward. Instead of asking *why them and not me?* I began asking, *what will I do with the life I have left?*

The truth is, none of us are guaranteed tomorrow. We don't know how much time we have—only how we choose to live with it. Survival isn't just about making it out alive; it's about learning to truly live after you do.

That is the lesson I had to learn.

And it is a lesson I am still learning.

The Unseen Battles in the Mind and Heart

The real war wasn't just the one fought outside with bullets and bombs—it was the one that continued inside me long after the attack had ended.

When the dust settled, and the world expected me to move forward, I found myself stuck in an invisible battlefield, one that no one could see but that I carried everywhere. Trauma doesn't disappear when the body is safe. It stays, reshaping the mind, tightening its grip when you least expect it.

The unseen battles of trauma are relentless. They come in waves—grief that strikes in the middle of a routine moment, guilt that whispers cruel questions, anger that burns hot and unrelenting.

Why them and not me?

How do I move forward when they never got the chance?

I should have been relieved to have survived, but instead, I felt trapped in a fog so thick that I didn't know how to break through. Survival came with a cost I hadn't anticipated—the loss of peace of mind. The feeling of safety had been stripped away, leaving me exposed to the unpredictability of life in a way I had never known before.

Everyone was looking for me to rise—family, friends, even colleagues who had seen me as the strong one. They reminded me of my resilience, of the things I had already overcome. They spoke of my faith, my strength, my ability to persevere. But what they couldn't see was that my spirit was curled up in a corner, unable to move.

Mondays became a dreadful day. Every new week felt like another battle I wasn't ready for. I put on a smile, I did my best to show up, but inside, I was barely hanging on. The nights were the hardest. Silence, once a comfort, had turned into something sinister. The absence of noise reminded me of the eerie stillness after the attack—the quiet that followed destruction.

Sleep became an elusive luxury. I laid in bed, staring at the ceiling, my mind replaying images I didn't want to see, hearing sounds I longed to forget. And so, I turned to what I thought would help—I relied on a glass of wine to soothe me to sleep. Then another. And another. Anything to quiet my thoughts, to slow my heartbeat, to feel even a fraction of normalcy.

But trauma doesn't work that way. It doesn't disappear because you ignore it, and it certainly doesn't fade because you drink it away. It embeds itself into the body—into the way your shoulders tense at sudden noises, the way your breath catches in crowded rooms, the way your heart races at the unexpected.

I wish I could say I immediately leaned into faith, that I found peace in scripture and prayer. But the truth is, my faith was shaken. My resolve was low. I wasn't angry at God—I was just lost. I didn't know how to reconcile my belief in His sovereignty with the weight of what I had survived. How do you trust fully when life has already proven how quickly everything can be taken away?

I didn't want this to be a story wrapped in a bow, a neat testimony of hardship overcome. Because the truth is, healing was a journey, and for a long time, I didn't feel like I was on the right path.

Yet, my journey mirrored one I would later reflect on—the story of Elijah in the wilderness (*1 Kings 19:1-13*). He, too, reached a breaking point. After all he had done, after witnessing miracles, he still fled, exhausted and overwhelmed, and asked God to take his life. But instead of responding with a grand display of power, God met him in a gentle whisper.

That was what faith became for me—not a loud, triumphant declaration, but a quiet, persistent whisper that told me to keep going.

Faith doesn't erase the pain. It doesn't undo the trauma. But it redefines the story.

Because trauma tries to convince you that you are trapped in the past, that you are defined by the worst thing that has ever happened to you.

But faith says otherwise.

Faith says there is more.

Faith says there is still life beyond the wreckage.

Faith says that even in the unseen battles, you are never fighting alone.

WHY ME?

Wrestling with Purpose in Pain

Confronting Survivor's Guilt

The question haunted me in the quiet moments.

Why me?

Why was I spared when others weren't? Why did I get to walk out of the bunker when others never got the chance?

Survivor's guilt is an unrelenting companion. It doesn't announce itself in grand displays of grief—it creeps in quietly, making itself known in the smallest moments. In the guilt that came with laughter. In the hesitation before taking a bite of food, knowing others would never have another meal. In the simple joy of sunlight on my face, accompanied by the whisper, *How dare you?*

The weight of loss sat heavy on my chest. I carried the names, the memories, the final places where friends had taken their last breaths. The gym where I had once found solace in movement had become a graveyard. The garden, where laughter once bloomed, was now a place of mourning. The restaurant, once filled with conversation and community, had become silent.

I was living among ghosts, and I didn't know how to make peace with it.

Empathy: The Heart of Survivor's Guilt

My empathy has always been my compass. It's why I chose the work I do—why I dedicated my life to advocating for those on the margins, fighting for justice, and amplifying the voices of those the world often silences. But the same empathy that fueled my passion for social impact also deepened my survivor's guilt.

I had spent my life witnessing suffering, not just in war zones but in the systemic injustices of the world—the cycles of poverty, the weight of racial discrimination, the communities left behind and forgotten. I had dedicated myself to standing alongside them, using my voice and skills to create change. But nothing prepared me for what it felt like to be on the other side of that loss—to be the one who had been spared.

I didn't just grieve my friends who died that night. I grieved for the women fighting for education in Afghanistan, the survivors of violence in Haiti, the children who may never know a world without struggle. My survival wasn't just mine—it was tied to so many stories that would never be told.

At times, I wanted to shrink under the weight of it all, to disappear into my grief, to not take up space in a world where others had been taken too soon.

But faith tells a different story.

Finding Meaning in the Pain

God doesn't keep us here by accident. Every breath is intentional.

There's a passage in Ecclesiastes 3:1-4 that says:

> *"There is a time for everything, and a season for every activity under the heavens: a time to be born and a time to die, a time to plant and a time to uproot, a time to kill and a time to heal,*

a time to tear down and a time to build, a time to weep and a time to laugh, a time to mourn and a time to dance."

I had been given a second chance—not because I was better, not because I was stronger, not because I was more deserving. But because my time wasn't up.

I was still here.

And that had to mean something.

For so long, I had believed my purpose was to serve others, to advocate for those who had been left behind. And yet, in the face of survival, I had to ask myself—what does it mean to be given another chance? What does it mean to honor the lives that were lost?

It meant I could no longer live small.

It meant I could no longer carry guilt instead of purpose.

It meant I had to live boldly, love fiercely, and fight even harder for those who were still here.

Survivor's guilt tells you that you should have been among the fallen. But faith tells you that because you are still here, your work is not done.

So I chose faith.

I chose to believe that my survival was not a burden, but a responsibility.

I chose to believe that my story was still unfolding, and that every day I was given was a chance to live in alignment with the purpose God had for me.

And so, I made a promise to myself and to those I had lost:

If I was going to live, then I would live fully.

I would love without hesitation.

I would fight without fear.

I would walk in my purpose, not with guilt, but with gratitude.

Because my survival was not just for me.

It was for every person I had ever fought for.

It was for those who would never get the chance to see another sunrise.

It was for something greater than myself.

And I would not waste it.

Seeking Meaning in Suffering

For a long time, I thought healing meant getting answers. That if I could just understand why God had spared me, I would find peace. But the truth is, some questions don't come with neat answers. Some pain doesn't resolve—it transforms.

My suffering wasn't wasted. It reshaped me. It forced me to live with intention, to stop treating time like an endless resource. It taught me to love harder, to embrace joy without guilt, to stop postponing the life I wanted to live.

But survival didn't just begin the night of the attack—it began long before that.

The Grit That Prepared Me for This Moment

I knew what it meant to defy the odds.

I grew up knowing struggle intimately—not just personal hardship, but the kind that comes from being born into systems designed to keep people like me on the margins. Poverty wasn't just an abstract concept; it was my reality. I attended one of the worst-performing high schools in New York City, a school where graduation was not an expectation but a rare victory. The statistics were stacked against me. Few made it out. Even fewer made it to college.

But grit is born in the fire.

I was raised in a world that told me my future was already decided, yet I refused to let it be written for me. By the grace of God, I went on to graduate from college, then earn a master's degree, and eventually, against every expectation placed upon me, I walked across the stage at the University of Southern California as Dr.—a title no system, no statistic, no barrier could take from me.

And my battles didn't start in the classroom.

As a child, I was diagnosed with lead poisoning, a condition that could have severely impacted my cognitive abilities. My mother was told that I might struggle, that learning disabilities could be in my future, that my potential was already capped before I had the chance to prove otherwise.

Yet, God had other plans.

What should have held me back became my fuel. Every limitation, every box society tried to put me in, only pushed me closer to faith. I had been fighting battles long before the attack on the compound—and just like before, God carried me through.

Pain as Preparation, Not Punishment

I used to think suffering was a punishment, something to be endured until it passed. But I now see that pain was also preparation.

James 1:2-4 says:

> *"Consider it pure joy, my brothers and sisters, whenever you face trials of many kinds, because you know that the testing of your faith produces perseverance. Let perseverance finish its work so that you may be mature and complete, not lacking anything."*

Perseverance is built in hardship. Resilience is refined in the struggle. And faith, the kind that can withstand storms, is forged in the moments when giving up seems like the easier choice.

I saw my survival as a second chance—an invitation to be fully present. I no longer wanted to move through life numb, as if I was merely existing. I wanted to feel everything deeply. To love without reservation. To take risks. To walk boldly in my purpose.

Romans 8:28 reminds us:

> *"And we know that in all things God works for the good of those who love Him, who have been called according to His purpose."*

It doesn't say that everything will be good. It doesn't promise that suffering won't come. But it assures us that God will take even our most painful moments and use them for something greater.

I began to ask a different question—not *Why me?* but *What now?*

What would I do with this life I had been given? How would I honor the ones who didn't get to see another day?

My survival was not just for me—it was a call to live with purpose.

Not a day passes that I don't remember the pain. But I refuse to let it define me. Instead, I choose to let it guide me—to walk in faith, to serve with an open heart, and to make every moment count.

Because if I have been given another chance at life, then I will live it fully.

And I will live it well.

What Is Your Bunker?

For me, the bunker was real—a physical place where life and death hung in the balance. The walls were made of concrete, the air was thick with fear, and the sound of gunfire echoed in the distance. But for many, the bunker is not a physical space. It is an emotional, spiritual, or mental stronghold—one that traps them just the same.

Maybe you have never had to hunch down in a bunker while the world exploded around you, but I promise you—you have faced a bunker of your own.

The Modern-Day Bunkers We Face

The bunker represents the moments of survival, where the weight of suffering, fear, and uncertainty press in so tightly that you don't know if you'll make it out. For some, it's a crisis of faith, a moment where you question if God sees you at all. For others, it's a season of suffering so intense that it feels like the walls are closing in.

Bunkers take many forms:

- **The Bunker of Addiction** – Maybe your battle is with alcohol, drugs, pornography, or destructive habits you swore you'd break free from. You promised yourself you wouldn't go back, but here you are, trapped again, stuck in a cycle that feels impossible to escape. You feel imprisoned by your own choices.

- **The Bunker of Depression and Anxiety** – The weight of sadness, panic, or hopelessness is so overwhelming that it's hard to get out of bed. You are physically here but mentally locked inside your own mind. The world continues around you, but you feel frozen, unable to move forward.

- **The Bunker of Toxic Relationships** -- Maybe it's a relationship that has drained you, broken you, made you feel less than who God created you to be. It could be an abusive marriage, an unhealthy friendship, or the inability to walk away from someone who continuously hurts you. You are trapped, knowing you need to leave but terrified of what's on the other side.

- **The Bunker of Shame and Regret** – Maybe it's something you did years ago, a mistake that still haunts you, a decision that cost you more than you ever imagined. You wear your past like a chain around your neck, convinced that if people really knew, they wouldn't see you the same way.

- **The Bunker of Incarceration** – Whether it's time spent behind bars or the lasting impact of a criminal record, incarceration creates an invisible prison long after the physical bars are gone. The system is designed to keep you trapped—not just physically, but emotionally, socially, and economically. You serve your time, yet society refuses to let you move forward. The weight of judgment, the struggle for a second chance, and the barriers to rebuilding your life make freedom feel like an illusion.

- **The Bunker of Financial Struggle** – You are doing everything you can, working long hours, cutting back, but the bills keep coming. You pray for provision, but every month, you feel like you're drowning. No matter how hard you work, you feel like you can't escape the weight of survival mode.

- **The Bunker of Grief and Loss** – You lost someone you loved—maybe to death, maybe to betrayal, maybe to time and distance. The emptiness they left behind is unbearable. The world tells you to move on, but how do you move forward when your heart is still stuck in the past?

- **The Bunker of Spiritual Warfare** – Maybe you feel like you're under attack—like every time you try to move forward, something drags you back. Doubt, temptation, fear, demonic oppression—every time you get close to a breakthrough, you feel resistance.

Does any of this sound familiar?

The bunker is that moment when fear grips you, when you can't see a way out, when it feels like you are just surviving, not living.

PART TWO

REBUILDING FROM THE RUBBLE

REBUILDING FROM THE RUBBLE

How Near-Death Moments Make You See Life Differently

In the bunker, I saw my life flash before my eyes—not in a chaotic blur, but in a way that felt deliberate and intentional. There was no panic, no frantic thoughts of unfinished business or regrets. I had lived fully, answered my calling, and given my best to the world. In those moments of uncertainty, I felt a quiet affirmation: Well done.

That sense of completeness followed me out of the bunker. When the gunfire stopped, when the dust settled, when I walked back into the world of the living, I carried with me a commitment—whatever added days I had left would be spent in gratitude, in intention, in presence.

But what does that really mean?

For some, near-death experiences send them searching for adrenaline. They chase thrill-seeking highs—skydiving, reckless decisions, extreme risks—because they are desperate to feel something, anything, after coming face-to-face with the fragility of life. Others lose themselves in distractions, unable to sit still, unable to be alone with their thoughts, unwilling to confront the weight of what they survived. But what I learned is that survival isn't about chasing the next thrill—it's about the power of presence.

The Power of Presence

Presence is often misunderstood. Some think it's just about being physically there, about showing up. But true presence —the kind that transforms your life—is about being fully engaged, fully aware, fully alive in the moment. It's about sitting in your own spirit and understanding that right now, in this moment, you are enough.

Survival has a way of forcing you to confront how much of life is lived on autopilot. How often do we go through the motions? Rushing from one thing to the next, barely absorbing the beauty around us, barely allowing ourselves to be present with the people we love?

A near-death experience strips away the illusion that time is endless. It teaches you that every moment is sacred. That every breath matters.

I had to learn how to live again—not just exist, not just function, but really live.

For me, that meant rethinking what it means to walk in faith. As a student of liberation theology, I have always understood faith as an active force, not a passive one. It is not just about endurance but about freedom. The early Black church understood this deeply. Despite their suffering, they did not let hardship be their only story. They built joy, community, and resistance in the face of oppression. They refused to let trauma be their only inheritance.

That's what I wanted my life to reflect. Not just the hardship, not just the survival, but the fullness of living—to create joy, to build memories, to see beauty, to love deeply, to exist in radical gratitude.

In many ways, presence is an act of defiance. To be fully present, fully engaged, fully grateful in a world that tries to steal your peace is an act of spiritual resistance.

For me, embracing presence meant slowing down. Listening more. Laughing harder. Holding space for both grief and joy without letting one erase the other. It meant being intentional with my time, knowing it's the most precious gift we have.

The Freedom of Gratitude

Gratitude changes everything. It takes survival and turns it into purpose. It turns "Why did I survive?" into "What will I do with this life I've been given?"

It reminds us, as James 4:14 says, that life is but a vapor—here for a moment and then gone. And because of that, we must *live fully, love deeply, and be present in the time we have.*

The early Black church didn't just preach about suffering; they preached about triumph in the face of suffering. About dancing even when the world tried to break them. Because to claim joy is to claim freedom.

That's what I want my life to reflect.

Not just survival. Not just pain. But the defiant act of being present—living now, embracing joy without guilt.

I have been given more time, and I refuse to waste it.

Surrendering Control

In today's world, we are taught to take control of our lives. We are told to drive, plan, direct, and orchestrate every detail—from our careers to our relationships, from our five-year plans to the smallest daily routines. We celebrate self-sufficiency, glorify ambition, and pride ourselves on being "in control" of our destinies.

Believers are not immune to this conditioning. In fact, we often bring this mindset into our relationship with God. We pray, but with expectations. We trust, but only if things align with our vision. We declare, *"Faith without works is dead,"* (James 2:26) but too often, we act as if we must orchestrate the outcome ourselves.

I remember having a deep conversation with a dear sister in our Millennials Ministry about how hard it is for us to truly let go and let God. We admitted how we often want God's will—as long as it looks like what we already had in mind. How we treat prayer as a means of confirmation, not surrender.

We laughed at our own stubbornness, knowing how often we wrestle with God instead of resting in Him.

Our deacon, ever so wise, checked us in the most gentle way.

"Are you seeking God's will, or are you seeking His agreement with you?"

That question sat with me. It still sits with me.

How many times have we asked for "God's guidance" when what we really wanted was His stamp of approval on the plans we already made? How often do we declare that God is in control—only to panic the moment things don't go our way?

Biblical Examples of the Illusion of Control

We are not the first to struggle with the illusion of control. Scripture is full of people—kings, prophets, rulers—who thought they were in charge, only to be reminded that God's sovereignty is absolute.

Pharaoh and the Exodus (Exodus 5-14) – Pharaoh believed he had full control over the Israelites. He ruled with an iron grip, convinced that his power was final. Even as Moses delivered message after message from God, Pharaoh's heart was hardened. He believed that his authority, his armies, his status as a god-king made him untouchable. But with every plague, God unraveled Pharaoh's illusion of control. And when the waters of the Red Sea swallowed his army, it became painfully clear—Pharaoh never had the power he thought he did.

Jonah's Flight (Jonah 1-4) – Jonah thought he could control his own obedience. God told him to go to Nineveh, but Jonah had other plans. He boarded a ship in the opposite direction, believing he could outrun God's will. But a storm, a fish, and three days in darkness taught him otherwise. Jonah had to learn the hard way—God's plan will prevail, with or without our cooperation.

Nebuchadnezzar's Humbling (Daniel 4:28-37) – King Nebuchadnezzar stood on the roof of his palace and declared, *"Is not this the great Babylon I have built as the royal residence, by my mighty power and for the glory of my majesty?"* (Daniel 4:30). He believed himself to be the master of his own success. But in an instant, God stripped him of his throne, his power, even his sanity. He was driven into the wilderness, living like a wild animal, until he finally acknowledged that God alone is sovereign.

These stories are more than historical accounts—they are reminders. God is in control, even when things don't go our way.

Trusting When the Path is Unclear

Letting go of control doesn't mean we stop making plans. It doesn't mean we sit idle and do nothing. It means we trust that God's plans are greater than our own.

Proverbs 19:21 says:

> *"Many are the plans in a person's heart, but it is the Lord's purpose that prevails."*

Faith is not about forcing our way—it's about aligning our will with His.

And surrender isn't passive. It's active. It's waking up every day and saying:

"Lord, I trust You even when I don't understand. I trust You even when my plans fail. I trust You even when the road ahead is unclear."

The night in the bunker taught me that I was never in control. And that's exactly why I was at peace.

God was in control then.

And He is in control now.

A Grateful Spirit

The Key to Inner Peace

Why Gratitude is a Weapon Against Despair

Gratitude is one of the most powerful spiritual disciplines, yet it is often misunderstood. Many think of gratitude as simply being thankful for good things, for answered prayers, for blessings that are easy to recognize. But true gratitude—the kind that sustains us, the kind that anchors us in the storms of life—is much deeper than that.

The Bible calls us to be grateful not just in seasons of abundance, but in all things:

> *"Give thanks in all circumstances; for this is God's will for you in Christ Jesus."* — 1 Thessalonians 5:18

That means gratitude is not just a response to good times; it is a posture we are called to hold, even in difficulty. Gratitude is a weapon. It is a direct rebellion against despair. It is the tool that keeps our spirits from sinking, the discipline that reminds us that even when life is hard, even when loss feels unbearable, there is still something worth holding onto.

But how does gratitude fight despair?

Because despair convinces you that you have nothing left. That everything has fallen apart. That joy is out of reach. But gratitude counters that lie. It reminds you that even in suffering, even in grief, there is still something to hold onto. Still breath in your lungs. Still warmth in the sun. Still kindness in the world.

Yet for many, gratitude feels abstract. How do we practice gratitude in a world that feels heavy? What does gratitude look like in real life?

Practicing Gratitude in a Modern World

In a world that moves fast, where we are constantly being told to chase more—more success, more possessions, more achievement—it can feel difficult to cultivate gratitude. We are conditioned to focus on what is missing instead of what is present.

But gratitude is not about ignoring pain or pretending that hardships don't exist. It is about shifting our focus. It is about training ourselves to see what is already here, rather than what is absent.

Practicing gratitude is:

- **Acknowledging the small victories**—waking up, making it through the day, having people who love you.

- **Giving thanks in prayer, even when things don't go your way.**

- **Being mindful of the present moment**—the sights, sounds, and sensations that we often overlook.

- **Recognizing the goodness in others**—choosing to see kindness instead of dwelling on negativity.

- **Choosing to find the lesson in hardships**—seeing how even difficulties shape and refine us.

Gratitude is not always a *feeling*—sometimes, it's a *discipline.* Some days, it will come naturally. Other days, you will have to choose to be grateful, even when nothing feels right.

But that is the very power of it.

Because when you choose gratitude, you starve despair. When you choose gratitude, you remind yourself that darkness does not get the final say.

Finding Joy in the Smallest Moments

One of the greatest lessons I've learned is that joy is not found in grand events or once-in-a-lifetime achievements. Joy lives in the smallest moments. The ones we often overlook. The ones we take for granted.

Even in the compound, under the constant threat of Taliban attack, I found joy.

I found joy in watching the butterflies kiss the flowers, delicate and fleeting. I found joy in letting the sun kiss my face, standing still, breathing in the warmth. Even in the uncertainty, even in the fear, I held onto those moments.

I found joy in the friendships I built with the other women on a mostly male-dominated camp. In the way we supported each other, how we laughed in between the heaviness, how we created a sense of home even in the most uncertain of places.

Joy is not just about laughter—it is about presence. It is about noticing the moments that make life worth living.

When you train yourself to see joy in the small things, despair loses its power. Because if you can find joy in the small things, then joy is never out of reach.

Jesus understood this deeply. He spoke of the sparrows that do not worry, yet are cared for (Matthew 6:26). He called us to be like children, unburdened, living in the moment (Matthew 18:3).

Joy is not a reward we earn; it is a gift we choose to receive.

And gratitude is the key that unlocks it.

So I choose gratitude. I choose to see joy. Even when life is hard. Even when the path is unclear. Because gratitude is not just a feeling—it is a way of life.

And when you choose to live in gratitude, despair never wins. What are you choosing?

FAITH IN ACTION

Walking Boldly Despite the Fear

Choosing Faith Over Fear in a Broken World

For many of us, the world feels like it is crumbling. The weight of injustice, war, oppression, and suffering is suffocating. We watch atrocities unfold in Haiti, Sudan, the Congo, Ukraine, and beyond, and we wonder: Where is God?

Here in the United States, we watch as Christianity is hijacked by white nationalists, twisted into a weapon for exclusion, bigotry, and domination. We hear their hateful rhetoric and think, "Not in our name."

And yet, we are not the first to ask where God is in the face of oppression.

The Israelites cried out under Pharaoh's rule. The enslaved Africans groaned under the weight of chattel slavery. The oppressed of every generation have called out to Yahweh, the God of Abraham, Isaac, and Jacob, pleading for justice. And every time, God has heard.

I know this because I have lived it.

That night in the bunker, I did not know if I would live or die. The gunfire, the explosions, the sheer weight of uncertainty—

it felt endless. In those long, agonizing hours, time lost all meaning, and I could have sworn that this was how my story would end.

But God had already written another chapter.

God delivered me.

Not because I was more righteous than those who didn't make it. Not because I had done anything special. But because He is sovereign, and my time was not yet up. And that experience changed the way I see everything.

Because when you are in the thick of suffering, it feels like there is no end. Like this is all there is. But my time in the bunker taught me that even when it seems like the darkness will last forever, deliverance is already on the horizon.

I walked out of that bunker forever changed—not just by the trauma of what I had endured, but by the clarity it gave me. The pain of survival made me see the suffering of others more deeply, not just as something to acknowledge but as something that connects us all.

Personal suffering and collective suffering are no different.

And just as God had His hand over me in that bunker, He has His hand over His people now.

The God who led me out of darkness is the same God who will lead His people through the struggles we face today.

We see this in Matthew 25:35-40, where Christ Himself makes it clear what His mission is:

> *"For I was hungry and you gave me something to eat, I was thirsty and you gave me something to drink, I was a stranger and you invited me in, I needed clothes and you clothed me, I was sick and you looked after me, I was in prison and you came to visit me."*

This is the heart of true Christianity—not power, not control, not nationalism, but care for the most vulnerable among us.

In a world that worships profit over people, where corporatists and oligarchs seek to hoard resources and amass power, faith becomes our greatest resistance. Choosing faith over fear means choosing to believe in God's justice when the world's justice system fails. It means knowing that Pharaoh's reign never lasts. That empires fall. That tyrants are brought low.

We do not have to look far in scripture to see this pattern.

- **Egypt's Pharaoh** ruled with an iron fist, but God drowned his armies in the Red Sea. (Exodus 14:26-28)

- **King Nebuchadnezzar** stood in arrogance, declaring his greatness, and God stripped him of his kingdom until he acknowledged divine authority. (Daniel 4:28-37)

- **The Tower of Babel** was built by people who sought to exalt themselves, but God scattered them and confused their language. (Genesis 11:1-9)

Those who believe they are untouchable will be humbled.

And yet, history repeats itself. We see modern pharaohs—political leaders who exploit the people, CEOs who build financial empires on the backs of the poor, and nationalist movements that claim divine favor while oppressing the very people Christ called us to serve. But Babylon does not last.

This is why we cannot afford to give in to fear.

To choose fear is to believe that the oppressors will win. But to choose faith is to believe in the same God who led the Israelites out of Egypt, who delivered His people time and time again, who hears the cries of the brokenhearted.

This is why liberation theology is so vital. It reminds us that God is not neutral in oppression—He is a God who sets captives free.

When enslaved Africans in the Americas cried for freedom, they weren't just pleading for earthly deliverance—they were calling on the God of Moses, of Miriam, of the Exodus. Just as God broke the yoke of slavery in Egypt, He would break the chains of transatlantic slavery.

Our God is a liberator.

And if we believe that, then we must live it.

While I speak from my own experience as a Black woman, a descendant of enslaved people, I know that oppression takes many forms. Some of you may carry the weight of generational poverty, the grip of addiction passed down like inheritance, or the pain of being cast aside in a world that devalues the vulnerable. Liberation is not just a historical event; it is an ongoing struggle that demands our collective commitment. If we truly believe in a God of justice, then we must stand against all systems that bind and break people, no matter what they look like or where they come from.

If we claim to follow a God who liberates, we, too, must be co-laborers in the liberation of ourselves and others.

Leaning Into Divine Strength When Human Strength Fails

We were never meant to fight these battles alone. The systems of power we are up against—whether political, economic, or spiritual—are too great for human strength alone. But we do not lean on human strength.

Paul reminds us in 2 Corinthians 12:9-10:

> *"My grace is sufficient for you, for my power is made perfect in weakness."*

When we feel powerless against the forces of evil in this world, when it seems like the oppressors are winning, we lean into divine strength.

- When Moses stood before the Red Sea, God made a way where there was none. (Exodus 14:21-22)

- When David stood before Goliath, it was not his strength, but the Lord's that won the battle. (1 Samuel 17:45-47)

- When Jesus stood before Pilate, the power of Rome meant nothing in the face of God's plan. (John 19:10-11)

This is what it means to walk in faith.

It means knowing that even when the world seems dark, we are not alone. That the same God who set captives free in Egypt, who humbled kings, who broke chains, is still moving today.

It means resisting the fear that tells us to give up. It means standing firm in the belief that justice will come, even if we do not see it in our lifetime. It means choosing faith even when the world mocks it, because we know whom we serve.

So when we look at the wars, the corruption, the violence, the suffering, we do not give in to despair.

Because we know who is really in control.

And it is not the rulers of this world.

PART THREE

LESSONS
FOR THE ROAD AHEAD

NAVIGATING AN UNCERTAIN WORLD WITH UNSHAKABLE FAITH

Lessons for Faith Believers in Difficult Times

We are living in unprecedented times, though history reminds us that every generation has felt the weight of its own storms. Wildfires rage uncontrollably, earthquakes shake the ground beneath us, hurricanes grow stronger, planes fall from the sky, and economic turmoil is testing the resilience of millions. The systems we have placed our trust in—our governments, economies, and institutions—are failing.

For many, fear is creeping in. Where is God in all of this?

But scripture reminds us that nothing is new under the sun (*Ecclesiastes 1:9*). We are not the first to experience chaos, nor will we be the last. The world has always been uncertain, but what separates faith believers from the rest of the world is how we respond.

Jesus warned us that these times would come:

> *"You will hear of wars and rumors of wars, but see to it that you are not alarmed. Such things must happen, but the end is still to come. Nation will rise against nation, and kingdom against kingdom. There will be famines and earthquakes in various places. All these are the beginning of birth pains."* — Matthew 24:6-8

The birth pains are a reminder that something is being ushered in. A shift is happening. And for those of us walking in faith, this is not the time to shrink back, but to prepare.

The lessons we take from this moment will determine how we navigate the road ahead.

1. **Recognizing Distractions & Guarding Your Spirit** – Social media, constant news cycles, endless entertainment—this generation is bombarded with noise. The world wants us busy, distracted, and numb. But faith requires presence. We cannot hear God if our minds are filled with everything else. We must be intentional about what we consume, what we prioritize, and what we allow to shape our hearts.

2. **Strengthening Discernment** – Not everything that sounds good is from God. False teachings, prosperity gospels, and ideologies that blend faith with nationalism or self-glorification are everywhere. Millennials and Gen Z have grown up skeptical—and rightly so. But we must learn the difference between being cautious and being disconnected from God's truth. Discernment comes from knowing His Word.

3. **Anchoring in Faith When the World is in Crisis** – The systems around us will fail. We are seeing it now. If our faith is tied to the economy, our careers, or human leaders, we will be shaken. But those whose faith is built on the Rock will stand (*Matthew 7:24-27*).

4. **Building a Prayer Life That Sustains You** – Too many of us have treated prayer as a last resort rather than our first line of defense. We cannot strengthen our faith in a crisis if we haven't built the habit in stillness. This season is a call to prepare. To pray not just in distress, but daily, as a way of staying connected to the source of our strength.

5. **Faith as a Daily Discipline, Not Just an Emotion** – We will not always *feel* strong. We will not always *feel* like praying. But faith is a commitment, not a feeling.

Just as we discipline ourselves to work, to exercise, or to pursue education, our spiritual lives require discipline too.

How to Anchor Yourself in Scripture and Prayer

A strong foundation of faith does not happen by accident. It is built with intention.

1. Prioritizing Time With God Over the Noise of the World

We make time for what we value. If we don't make time for God, the world will quickly fill that space with something else. Set aside time daily—whether in the morning, before bed, or during lunch—to read scripture and pray.

"But seek first His kingdom and His righteousness, and all these things will be given to you as well." — Matthew 6:33

2. Developing a Scripture-Based Faith (Not a Social Media Faith)

In an age of Instagram theology and TikTok spirituality, many have formed their beliefs from 30-second soundbites rather than the Word itself. We cannot afford a surface-level faith. We must go deeper.

"Your word is a lamp for my feet, a light on my path." — Psalm 119:105

Start with these foundational scriptures:

- **For Strength in Trials:** *James 1:2-4*
- **For Overcoming Fear:** *2 Timothy 1:7*
- **For God's Provision:** *Philippians 4:19*
- **For When You Feel Weary:** *Isaiah 40:31*

3. Learning to Pray Boldly and Expectantly

Prayer is not just a ritual—it is our direct connection to God. Yet, so many of us struggle with it. We overcomplicate it, thinking we need the right words, the perfect setting, or the right emotions.

Jesus gave us the Lord's Prayer (*Matthew 6:9-13*) as a model, but He also showed us that prayer is about relationship, not performance.

4. Surrounding Yourself With a Community of Believers

Faith is not meant to be walked alone. In difficult times, the enemy works to isolate us, making us think no one understands our struggles. But scripture constantly emphasizes community.

> *"As iron sharpens iron, so one person sharpens another."* — Proverbs 27:17

Find a church, a small group, or mentors who will hold you accountable, pray with you, and remind you of God's truth when you begin to doubt.

5. Choosing Faith Over Fear in Uncertain Times

At the core of it all, fear will try to silence our faith. The news, social media, world events—all of it fuels fear. But God did not call us to live in fear.

> *"For God has not given us a spirit of fear, but of power, love, and a sound mind."* — 2 Timothy 1:7

Fear says, **"Everything is falling apart."**

Faith says, **"God is still in control."**

Fear says, **"There is no way out."**

Faith says, **"God will make a way."**

Fear says, **"You are not strong enough."**

Faith says, **"God's strength is made perfect in weakness."** (*2 Corinthians 12:9*)

The Call to Strengthen Your Faith Now

We are standing at a pivotal moment in history. The world is shifting, and those who are unprepared will be swept away by the noise, the chaos, and the confusion.

But those who have anchored themselves in God's Word, in prayer, in community, and in faith will not be shaken.

This is a call to action.

This is a warning and an invitation.

Now is the time to strengthen your faith. Not tomorrow. Not when another crisis hits. Now.

Because when the world shakes again—and it will shake again—your foundation must already be built.

Will you be ready?

THE GIFT OF NOW

How the Present Heals the Past and Prepares the Future

The Danger of Dwelling in Past Trauma

Trauma has a way of trapping us in time. It keeps us reliving the moment of pain, betrayal, loss, or fear. The past becomes a loop—one we can't seem to escape.

For me, my "bunker moment" was not just the night of the attack—it was the aftermath. The months of sleepless nights, the survivor's guilt, the moments where I felt like I was floating through life without feeling truly alive.

I had escaped the physical bunker, but mentally, emotionally, and spiritually, I was still trapped inside it.

For many, their trauma does not come from war zones but from childhood wounds, abuse, loss, violence, systemic oppression, or personal failures. The bunker is different for each of us, but the impact is the same—it keeps us from living fully in the present.

Dwelling in past trauma is dangerous because:

- **It robs us of the present** – We are so consumed by what was that we fail to see what is.

- **It distorts our identity** – We start defining ourselves by our wounds rather than by the healing God has for us.

- **It isolates us** – Shame, fear, and unresolved pain make us withdraw from relationships and support.

- **It convinces us that we will never be whole again** – Trauma tells us that we are broken beyond repair.

But God does not call us to live in the past. He calls us to step forward, to trust that healing is possible, and to surrender our burdens daily.

Prayer is Part of the Healing—Not a Replacement for It

This is **not** a book about *praying trauma away*.

I believe in prayer, but prayer is not a substitute for healing—it is part of the healing. Just as we trust doctors for physical illnesses, we must recognize that trauma is both a spiritual and psychological wound—one that requires faith and therapy.

To address my PTSD, I sought therapy in a space that honored all parts of my identity—my faith, my cultural background, my experiences. Therapy gave me the language to understand my trauma, but faith gave me the strength to move through it.

This is why Christian Trauma Therapy can be such a powerful tool. It does not dismiss science or mental health—it integrates faith with therapeutic healing. It acknowledges:

- **The spiritual wounds caused by trauma** – How our suffering shapes our relationship with God and others.

- **The emotional and physiological impact** – How trauma rewires the brain and body.

- **The power of Scripture in healing** – Using biblical truths to combat lies trauma tells us.

There is literature supporting faith-based trauma healing, and more Christians are recognizing that seeking help is not a lack of faith—it is a step of faith.

"The Lord is close to the brokenhearted and saves those who are crushed in spirit." — Psalm 34:18

God does not expect us to heal alone. He gives us tools—prayer, therapy, community, and His Word—to rebuild what was broken.

Moving Past Trauma: Your Support System Matters

No one heals alone.

When I look back at my healing journey, I see the hands that pulled me through—mentors, friends, therapists, my church family, my faith. The bunker felt isolating, but in reality, God had placed people in my life to walk with me.

The same is true for you.

If you are still trapped in your trauma, still waking up with a heavy heart, you do not have to walk alone.

Here are ways to lean on your support system:

1. **Find a therapist who honors your faith** – Christian Trauma Therapy integrates faith with psychological healing. There are several other well-respected Christian therapy models that address trauma while integrating faith-based approaches. Find what works best for you.

2. **Join a faith-based support group** – Healing happens in community, not isolation.

3. **Seek wise counsel** – Find mentors or elders in your church who will walk with you.

4. **Let people in** – Healing requires vulnerability. Let trusted friends and family know what you need.

5. **Commit to the process** – Healing is not linear. It takes time, but every step forward is a step toward freedom.

"Carry each other's burdens, and in this way, you will fulfill the law of Christ." — Galatians 6:2

God designed us for community. Healing requires connection.

The Practice of Daily Surrender and Trust

One of the hardest lessons I had to learn was how to surrender daily.

Not just once. Not just on Sundays. Every. Single. Day.

Because trauma tries to return. The thoughts, the memories, the fear—they creep back in. The only way to move forward is to practice surrender as a discipline, not just an emotion.

So what does **daily surrender look like when all feels lost?**

1. **Starting the day with prayer and truth** – Before the world gets loud, anchor yourself in God's promises.

2. **Speaking life over yourself** – Trauma tells us we are broken. Speak what God says instead.

3. **Releasing what you cannot control** – Fear thrives in control. Trust God with what you cannot fix today.

4. **Ending the day in gratitude** – Even on hard days, find something to thank God for.

"Come to me, all you who are weary and burdened, and I will give you rest." — Matthew 11:28

Daily surrender does not erase the past, but it keeps it from controlling your future.

Healing is a journey. **But you do not have to stay in the bunker forever.**

The present—right now—is where healing begins.

What Surviving Taught Me About True Freedom

Freedom from Fear, Bitterness, and Regret

Survival does not just change you—it forces you to make a choice.

When I walked out of that bunker, I could have chosen bitterness—bitterness toward Afghanistan, toward the people, toward the war that had uprooted so many lives. I could have let the Taliban attack harden my heart, making me resentful and filled with hate.

I could have chosen anger—anger at the U.S. government for failing to protect me, for getting in too deep in a war it could not control, for sending civilians into a conflict it barely understood.

I could have chosen regret—regret for ever accepting the position, for stepping into dangerous territory, for putting my life on the line for something that, in the grand scheme of politics, I had no power to change.

But I chose none of those things.

Because fear, bitterness, and regret are chains just as powerful as any physical prison. And true freedom—the kind that comes from faith—means choosing not to be bound by them.

I understood that the war that had fueled the attack was not personal—it was systemic. It was about power, profit, control, and cycles of violence too deep-rooted for one person to dismantle. The people who had carried out the attack were also caught in something bigger than themselves. Hate was the easy option, but it was not the answer.

Regret would not have served me, because if I truly believed that God was guiding my steps, then I had to believe I was always at the right place at the right time.

The same is true for you.

No matter what your bunker looks like—whether it's betrayal, trauma, loss, or hardship—you have a choice.

You can choose to be bitter about what happened.

You can choose to regret every decision that led you here.

Or you can choose to trust that even this—yes, even this—is part of something greater.

How Crisis Redefines Priorities and Purpose

When we experience crisis, we often see it as a moment of disruption—something that takes us off course, something that ruins what we were trying to build.

But what if crisis is not a detour, but a refinement?

Look at the story of the Israelites and Egypt.

- They were enslaved under Pharaoh, crying out for deliverance. (Exodus 3:7)

- God sent Moses to lead them to freedom, performing miracle after miracle to set them loose. (Exodus 12:31-42)

- But when they got to the wilderness—when they had been freed from their oppressors—many of them wanted to go back. (Exodus 16:3)

They longed for the familiarity of Egypt, even though Egypt had been their place of bondage.

This is what crisis does. It forces us to choose.

- Will we step into faith, or will we long for the security of our past—even when our past was hurting us?
- Will we trust that God is taking us somewhere greater, or will we resist Him because the road ahead looks uncertain?

Some of the same Israelites who were once enslaved became oppressors themselves. They forgot what it was like to suffer and chose to build their own power rather than follow God's ways.

We see the same patterns in the world today. How many of us, once we get free, begin to act just like the ones we were once fleeing?

Crisis reveals our hearts. It shows us who we are.

So what will you choose?

Will your pain make you bitter, or will it make you wiser?
Will your hardship fill you with fear, or will it strengthen your faith?
Will you cling to regret, or will you trust that God is still moving?

A Guide for Others Walking Through Their Own Crisis

If you're in a crisis, if you're facing your own bunker moment, know this—this is not the end of your story.

Here's how you can avoid the traps of fear, bitterness, and regret and step into true freedom.

1. Acknowledge the Pain, But Don't Become It

What happened to you was real. It was painful. It was unfair. But it does not have to define the rest of your life. Let yourself feel, but do not let those feelings become permanent chains.

2. Choose Faith Over Bitterness

Bitterness tells you that you were wronged, and maybe you were. But bitterness doesn't change the past—it only poisons your future. Faith says, *"God, I don't understand, but I trust You."*

3. Don't Regret, Reflect

Regret keeps you stuck. Reflection moves you forward. Instead of asking *"Why did this happen to me?"*, ask *"What is God teaching me through this?"*

4. Make Purpose Out of Pain

Every crisis brings clarity. It strips away the unnecessary and reveals what actually matters. What has your crisis taught you? What needs to change in your life? What is God calling you to now?

5. Stay Focused on the Future

Egypt was a place of captivity, but God was calling the Israelites to the Promised Land. Don't let temporary hardship make you forget that God has more for you ahead.

6. Remember Who is Really in Control

The world is chaotic. War, oppression, systems of power, personal loss—all of it can make us feel powerless. But the kingdoms of this world are temporary. Governments fall. Leaders change. Wealth disappears. Only God remains.

The Lord foils the plans of the nations; He thwarts the purposes of the peoples. But the plans of the Lord stand firm forever, the purposes of His heart through all generations. — Psalm 33:10-11

CONCLUSION

Down in the Bunker, But Not Defeated

There was a moment, deep in that bunker, when I thought my story was ending. The walls felt too tight, the fear too overwhelming, the uncertainty too vast. I had no power over what was happening outside. No control over whether I would make it out alive to ever see my babies. All I could do was pray, breathe, and wait.

But what I didn't know then was that the bunker wasn't my end—it was my beginning.

The world will tell you that survival is about physical endurance, about making it through the night. But I have learned that true survival is about learning to live again after the storm has passed. It is about stepping out of the bunker—physically, emotionally, spiritually, and mentally.

The bunker was never just about a physical place. It is the space where fear grips you, where you question everything, where you wonder if you will ever be whole again. It is the waiting place, the holding place, the place where the battle between despair and faith is waged.

Maybe your bunker is a season of loss—the grief of losing someone you love, the weight of shattered dreams, the agony of an ending you never expected.

Maybe your bunker is **a crisis of faith**—a moment where everything you thought you believed feels uncertain, and you wonder if God is still with you.

Maybe your bunker is **a battle with trauma**—the memories that won't leave, the nights that stretch too long, the echoes of pain that refuse to fade.

Maybe your bunker is **fear of the future**—the anxiety of what comes next, the overwhelming feeling that you are not enough, the doubts that creep into the quiet moments.

Whatever your bunker is, I want you to know this—you are not alone.

I came out of that bunker knowing that my survival was not just for me—it was so I could tell this story. It was so I could remind you that there is life beyond the pain, that there is hope beyond the darkness, that there is a God who never leaves, even when everything else falls apart.

Recognizing and Rising from Your Own Bunker

To those of you who are still in the bunker, still waiting, still unsure of what comes next—hold on.

The night may feel endless, but the dawn always comes.

You may feel trapped now, but this is not where your story ends.

You may not see the way forward, but God does.

He was with me in the bunker, just as He was with Daniel in the lions' den, with Paul and Silas in prison, with Shadrach, Meshach, and Abednego in the fire. And He is with you now.

The bunker is not your final destination—it is the place where your faith is being refined. It is the place where you will discover what you are truly made of. It is the place where God is preparing you for the life that is still ahead of you.

So do not let fear define you. Do not let despair consume you. Do not let the darkness convince you that the light is gone.

You are still here for a reason.

Even in Our Darkest Moments, Light is Present

Throughout scripture, God has always used the darkest moments to reveal His power. He is the God of liberation, the God of justice, the God of redemption.

- When the Israelites cried out under **Pharaoh's oppression**, He parted the Red Sea and set them free.
- When **Elijah fled into the wilderness**, exhausted and ready to give up, God met him—not in the fire, not in the wind, but in a whisper.
- When **the disciples panicked in the storm**, Jesus stood and rebuked the wind, reminding them that faith, not fear, should be their anchor.

Even on the darkest night, light is present.

Even in the deepest suffering, hope is alive.

Even when it feels like all is lost, God is still moving.

That is the truth I carried out of the bunker. That is the truth I want to leave you with.

Your pain is not meaningless. Your suffering is not wasted.

If you are still here, then God is not done with you yet.

So walk forward, not in fear, but in faith.

Live boldly. Love deeply. And make every moment count.

Because you may have been down in the bunker—but you are not defeated.

And by God's grace, you never will be.

Rebuilding
After the Bunker

A Guide to Restoration and Grace

The journey out of the bunker—whether it is emotional, spiritual, or physical—requires faith, courage, and grace. This guide will help you move forward step by step. Each section includes a reflection, journal prompt, and prayer to deepen your healing process.

Step 1 – Recognize the Bunker: Naming the Trauma

The Lord is close to the brokenhearted and saves those who are crushed in spirit. — Psalm 34:18

Reflection

Before you can rebuild, you must acknowledge the bunker you have been living in. Maybe it was a season of fear, grief, or self-protection. Naming it brings clarity.

Journal Prompt

- What is my bunker? (Fear, trauma, loss, control, anger, disappointment?)
- How has staying in this place helped or harmed me?

Prayer for Awareness

God, show me the walls I have built around my heart. Reveal where I have been hiding, and give me the courage to step into healing. You are near to the brokenhearted—help me to believe that includes me.

Step 2 – Let in the Light: Seeking Hope and Truth

Then you will know the truth, and the truth will set you free.
— John 8:32

Reflection

Lies often keep us in the bunker—lies about our worth, our future, or even God's love. Truth is the key that unlocks the door to freedom.

Journal Prompt

- What false beliefs have I carried from my trauma?
- What truth from God's Word can replace these lies?

Prayer for Truth

Father, I surrender every lie I have believed. Replace my fear with faith, my shame with grace, and my doubt with hope. Open my eyes to Your truth. Amen.

Step 3 – Strengthen the Foundation: Rebuilding Faith and Identity

Everyone who hears these words of mine and puts them into practice is like a wise man who built his house on the rock. — Matthew 7:24

Reflection

Once the bunker walls come down, what will you build your life upon? Faith is the only foundation strong enough to withstand life's storms.

Journal Prompt

- What are three core truths I want to build my life on?
- How can I strengthen my faith daily?

Prayer for a Stronger Foundation

Lord, I choose to build my life on You. Teach me to stand firm in faith, to trust Your Word, and to walk in Your strength. Be my firm foundation. Amen.

Step 4 – Clear the Rubble: Forgiveness and Letting Go

Forget the former things; do not dwell on the past.
See, I am doing a new thing! — Isaiah 43:18-19

Reflection

You cannot build on a foundation covered in rubble. Forgiveness is a form of spiritual demolition—it clears the way for new beginnings.

Journal Prompt

- What pain, resentment, or regret am I holding onto?
- Who or what do I need to forgive to move forward?

Prayer for Letting Go

Jesus, I release the weight of my past. I choose to forgive—even when it's hard—because You have forgiven me. Free me from bitterness and make room for new beginnings. Amen.

Step 5 – Build a Support Network: Healing in Community

Two are better than one… If either of them falls, one can help the other up. — Ecclesiastes 4:9-10

Reflection

Healing does not happen in isolation. God uses people— mentors, friends, and church communities—to help us rebuild.

Journal Prompt

- Who are the people I can rely on for encouragement and accountability?

- What step can I take this week to invest in meaningful relationships?

Prayer for Community

Lord, send the right people into my life—those who will pray with me, encourage me, and challenge me to grow. Help me to be that person for others, too. Amen.

Step 6 – Walk in Purpose:
Discovering a New Mission After Pain

And we know that in all things God works for the good of those who love Him. — Romans 8:28

Reflection

Your pain is not wasted. God can turn your bunker season into a story of redemption—not just for you but for others.

Journal Prompt

- How has my experience shaped my calling or purpose?
- How can I use my story to help someone else?

Prayer for Purpose

Father, take what the enemy meant for harm and use it for good. Show me how to use my story for Your glory. Amen.

Step 7 – Live in Grace: Sustaining Faith and Growth

My grace is sufficient for you, for My power is made perfect in weakness. — 2 Corinthians 12:9

Reflection

Healing is an ongoing journey. Some days you will feel strong, and some days you will struggle. Grace is what keeps you moving forward.

Journal Prompt

- What does grace mean to me in this season?
- What spiritual practices will help me stay anchored in faith?

Prayer for Grace

Lord, when I fall, remind me that Your grace is enough. When I doubt, remind me that Your love never fails. Help me to walk forward in faith, one day at a time. Amen.

DISCUSSION GROUP GUIDE

This guide is designed to help groups process, reflect, and grow together through the themes in *Down in the Bunker*. Each session includes a key scripture, discussion questions, and an optional group activity to deepen engagement. Groups can meet weekly or adjust the pacing to fit their schedule.

Session 1 – Recognizing the Bunker

The Lord is close to the brokenhearted and saves those who are crushed in spirit. — Psalm 34:18

Discussion Questions

1. What does "the bunker" represent in your life?

2. Have there been times when you have isolated yourself spiritually, emotionally, or physically? What led you to that place?

3. How does God meet us in our moments of brokenness?

4. What fears hold you back from stepping out of your bunker?

Group Activity

As a group, take a few moments to write down one area where you feel stuck. Then, pray collectively for God's grace to bring light into those places.

Session 2 – Letting in the Light

Then you will know the truth, and the truth will set you free.
— John 8:32

Discussion Questions

1. What lies have you believed about yourself, your worth, or God's love?

2. How does replacing lies with biblical truth bring healing?

3. What scriptures or promises from God have helped you overcome past struggles?

4. How can we, as a faith community, help one another walk in truth?

Group Activity

Have each person write down a negative belief they struggle with. Then, find and share a Bible verse that speaks truth into that situation. Encourage members to replace the negative belief with the scripture throughout the week.

Session 3 – Rebuilding on a Firm Foundation

Everyone who hears these words of mine and puts them into practice is like a wise man who built his house on the rock. — Matthew 7:24

Discussion Questions

1. What are the foundations in your life? Are they strong, or do they feel shaky?

2. How do we practically build our faith so that it can sustain us through challenges?

3. What are some spiritual disciplines (prayer, fasting, scripture reading) that have helped you grow in faith?

4. When life becomes overwhelming, how can we remind ourselves of God's firm foundation?

Group Activity

As a group, create a "Faith Foundation List." Each person shares one truth, practice, or scripture that has anchored them in difficult times. Write them down and distribute them to group members as encouragement.

Session 4 – Clearing the Rubble

Forget the former things; do not dwell on the past. See, I am doing a new thing! — Isaiah 43:18-19

Discussion Questions

1. What are some areas of your life where you feel weighed down by past hurts?

2. How does unforgiveness keep us trapped in the past?

3. What is one step you can take toward forgiveness— even if the hurt feels fresh?

4. What role does God's grace play in helping us let go of resentment?

Group Activity

If comfortable, have each person write a letter of forgiveness (to themselves, to others, or to God). They do not have to share it aloud. End with a time of prayer for freedom and healing.

Session 5 – Healing in Community

*Two are better than one… If either of them falls,
one can help the other up.* — Ecclesiastes 4:9-10

Discussion Questions

1. Why is it hard to ask for help or lean on others during difficult times?

2. What role does the Christian community play in our healing process?

3. How can we become safe spaces for one another to share struggles?

4. What is one way you can be a source of encouragement for someone this week?

Group Activity

Pair up and commit to checking in with one another throughout the next week. Whether through prayer, a text message, or a phone call, stay connected and offer encouragement.

Session 6 – Finding Purpose After the Storm

And we know that in all things God works for the good of those who love Him. — Romans 8:28

Discussion Questions

1. What is one lesson you've learned through a painful experience?

2. How can God use your story to encourage others?

3. How does trusting in God's purpose help bring peace to our past?

4. What is one way you can take a step toward using your experiences for good?

Group Activity

Each person writes down one talent, experience, or lesson God has given them. Discuss how these can be used to serve others.

Session 7 – Sustaining Growth and Walking in Grace

My grace is sufficient for you,
for My power is made perfect in weakness. — 2 Corinthians 12:9

Discussion Questions

1. How can we remind ourselves daily that God's grace is enough?

2. When old fears or struggles resurface, what practices help you stay strong in faith?

3. What does it mean to walk in grace, not perfection?

4. How can we continue growing spiritually after this study ends?

Group Activity

End with a group prayer and a time of commitment. Have each person share one key takeaway from this study and how they plan to apply it moving forward.

Encouragement for Group Leaders

Encourage members to continue their healing and faith journey beyond this study. Here are a few ways to keep the momentum going:

- Start a prayer partner system where members check in regularly.

- Continue meeting for fellowship and discussion on other faith-based books.

- Encourage journaling or daily scripture reading to reinforce spiritual growth.

- Organize a group service project to turn healing into action.

For those interested in going deeper, consider reading additional books on faith and resilience, or participating in church workshops and retreats.

SCRIPTURE REFERENCE GUIDE FOR REFLECTION & STUDY

The following scriptures have been referenced throughout this book. Whether you are seeking strength, healing, or a reminder of God's presence, use this guide as a tool for reflection and encouragement.

Faith in the Fire

- Daniel 3:16-27
- Isaiah 43:2
- Job 13:15
- Matthew 7:24-27

Overcoming Fear & Finding Strength

- Psalm 27:1
- Isaiah 40:31
- 2 Timothy 1:7
- Mark 4:35-41

God's Protection & Deliverance

- Daniel 6:16-23

- Exodus 14:21-22
- Acts 16:25-26
- Psalm 23:4

Walking in God's Grace

- 2 Corinthians 12:9
- Romans 8:28
- Psalm 34:18
- Matthew 6:33

Trusting God's Plan

- Proverbs 19:21
- Psalm 33:10-11
- Matthew 24:6-8
- Ecclesiastes 3:1-4

Serving Others

- Matthew 25:35-40
- Galatians 6:2
- James 2:26

God's Word as Guidance

- Psalm 119:105
- John 8:32
- Matthew 6:9-13
- Proverbs 27:17

Which scripture spoke to you the most? Consider journaling about it or sharing your thoughts with a friend.

If this book encouraged you, I'd love to hear how it impacted your faith journey.

About the Author

Dr. Lovesun Parent is a survivor, writer, and advocate for social inclusion and global healing. Her journey has taken her from the streets of New York City to the frontlines of humanitarian work, where she has worked to uplift marginalized communities, particularly women and girls. But her deepest lessons came after surviving a harrowing attack—learning that survival isn't just about making it out alive but about finding the strength to truly live again.

Through faith, therapy, and reflection, she navigated the complexities of trauma and resilience, realizing that healing is both a spiritual and practical journey. This book is her offering to those facing their own "bunkers"—a reminder that even in life's darkest moments, hope is never lost.

When she's not writing or advocating for marginalized communities, she's finding new ways to soak up the world around her—whether basking in the sun, stumbling upon something beautiful in nature, or laughing way too loud with loved ones. She believes in joy as an act of resistance, faith as a tool for survival, and storytelling as a way to bring healing to the world.

A Note from the Author

Thank you for joining me on this healing journey. My hope is that *Down in the Bunker* has encouraged you to hold on to grace in the midst of chaos. If this book resonated with you, I'd love to hear your thoughts!

How You Can Help

- Leave a review on Amazon, Goodreads, or wherever books are sold—your words help others find this message of faith.

- Connect with me on social media @dr.loveparent.

- Share this book with a friend or your church group—faith grows when we walk together.

Coming Soon!

Look out for *Not in Our Name: Reclaiming the Gospel from Extremism*, where I challenge the hijacking of Christianity for hate and exclusion, reclaiming its true message of justice, compassion, and liberation. Stay tuned!

With gratitude,
Dr. Lovesun Parent